ENGLISH/JAPANESE

The T♡ddler's handb◉◉k

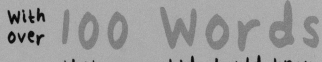

with over **100 Words** that every kid should know

BY DAYNA MARTIN

えいご / にほんご

ENGAGE BOOKS
VANCOUVER

1

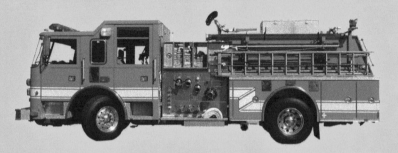

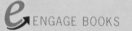

Mailing address
PO BOX 4608
Main Station Terminal
349 West Georgia Street
Vancouver, BC
Canada, V6B 4A1

www.engagebooks.ca

Written & compiled by: Dayna Martin
Edited & designed by: A.R. Roumanis
Translated by: Miz Hashimoto はしもとみず
Photos supplied by: Shutterstock
Photo on page 47 by: Faye Cornish

FIRST EDITION / FIRST PRINTING

LIBRARY AND ARCHIVES CANADA CATALOGUING IN PUBLICATION

Martin, Dayna, 1983–, author
    The toddler's handbook : numbers, colors, shapes, sizes, ABC animals, opposites, and sounds, with over 100 words that every kid should know / written by Dayna Martin ; edited by A.R. Roumanis.

Issued in print and electronic formats.
Text in English and Japanese.
ISBN 978-1-77226-473-9 (bound). –
ISBN 978-1-77226-474-6 (paperback). –
ISBN 978-1-77226-475-3 (pdf). –
ISBN 978-1-77226-476-0 (epub). –
ISBN 978-1-77226-477-7 (kindle)

1. Chinese language – Vocabulary – Juvenile literature.
2. Vocabulary – Juvenile literature.
I. Martin, Dayna, 1983– . Toddler's handbook.
II. Martin, Dayna, 1983– . Toddler's handbook. Japanese.
III. Title.

PL642.M37 2017   J491.4'381   C2017-905774-X
                                        C2017-905775-8

るふぁべっと
Arufabetto
4
ABCs

すうじ
Sūji
11
Numbers

いろ
Iro
14
Colors

はんたいご
Hantaikotoba
16
Opposites

かたち
Katachi
22
Shapes

おと
Oto
24
Sounds

こうどう
Kōdō
28
Actions

かんじょう
Kanjō
30
Emotions

すぽーつ
Supōtsu
32
Sports

のりもの
Norimono
34
Engines

おおきさ
Oki-sa
36
Sizes

からだ
Karada
38
Body

しょっき
Shokki
40
Tableware

ふく
Fuku
42
Clothes

おふろのじかん
O furo noji ka n
44
Bath Time

ねるじかん
Neruji ka n
45
Bed Time
3

ありげーたー

Arigētā

Aa

Alligator

くま

Kuma

Bb

4 **Bear**

ねこ

Neko

Cc

Cat

いぬ

Inu

Dd

Dog

ぞう

Zō

Ee

Elephant

きつね

Kitsune

Ff

Fox

やぎ

Yagi

Gg

Goat 5

うま
Uma

Hh

Horse

いぐあな
Iguana

Ii

Iguana

じゃがー
Jagā

Jj

Jaguar

6

こあら
Koara

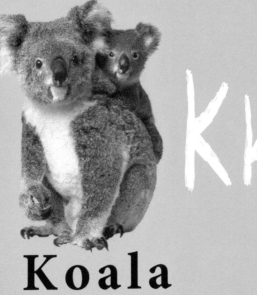

Kk

Koala

らいおん
Raion

Ll

Lion

ねずみ
Nezumi

Mm

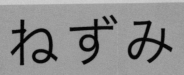

Mouse

にゅーと
Ni~yuto

Nn

Newt 7

かわうそ
Kawauso

Oo

Otter

ぶた
Buta

Pp

Pig

うずら
Uzura

Qq

Quail

うさぎ
Usagi

Rr

Rabbit

あざらし
Azarashi

Ss

Seal

とら
Tora

Tt

Tiger

うあかり
Uakari

Uu

Uakari

こんどる
Kondoru

Vv

Vulture 9

いたち
Itachi

Ww

Weasel

Xせんさかな
X-sen sakana

Xx

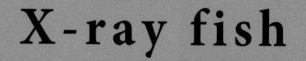

X-ray fish

やく
Yaku

Yy

10 **Yak**

しまうま
Shimauma

Zz

Zebra

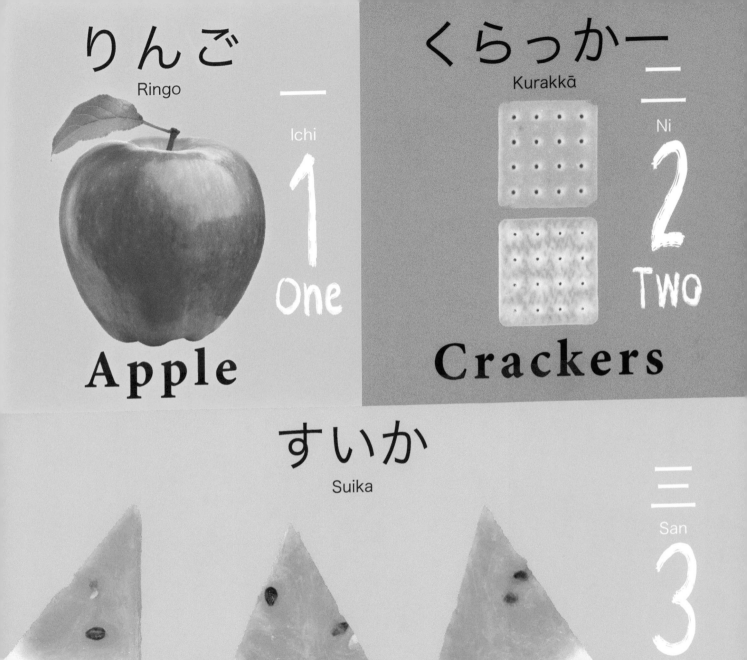

りんご

Ringo

一

Ichi

1

One

Apple

くらっかー

Kurakkā

二

Ni

2

Two

Crackers

すいか

Suika

三

San

3

Three

Watermelon slices

四
Shi

いちご
Ichigo

4
Four

Strawberries

五
Go

にんじん
Ninjin

5
Five

Carrots

六
Roku

6
Six

とまと
Tomato

12

Tomatoes

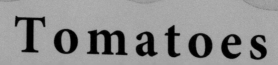

かぼちゃ
Kabocha

七
Shichi

7
Seven

Pumpkins

くだもの
Kudamono

八
Hachi

8
Eight

Fruit slices

じゃがいも
Jagaimo

九
kyū

9
Nine

Potatoes

くっきー
Kukkī

十
Jū

10
Ten

Cookies 13

にじ
Niji

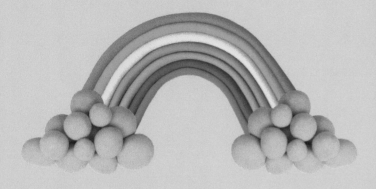

Rainbow

あか
Aka

Red

おれんじ
Orenji

14 Orange

きいろ
Kīro

Yellow

みどり
Midori

Green

あお
Ao

Blue

あいいろ
Aiiro

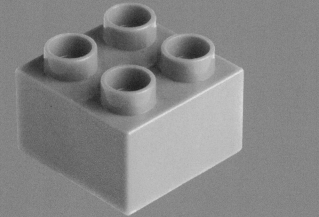

Indigo

むらさき
Murasaki

Violet

15

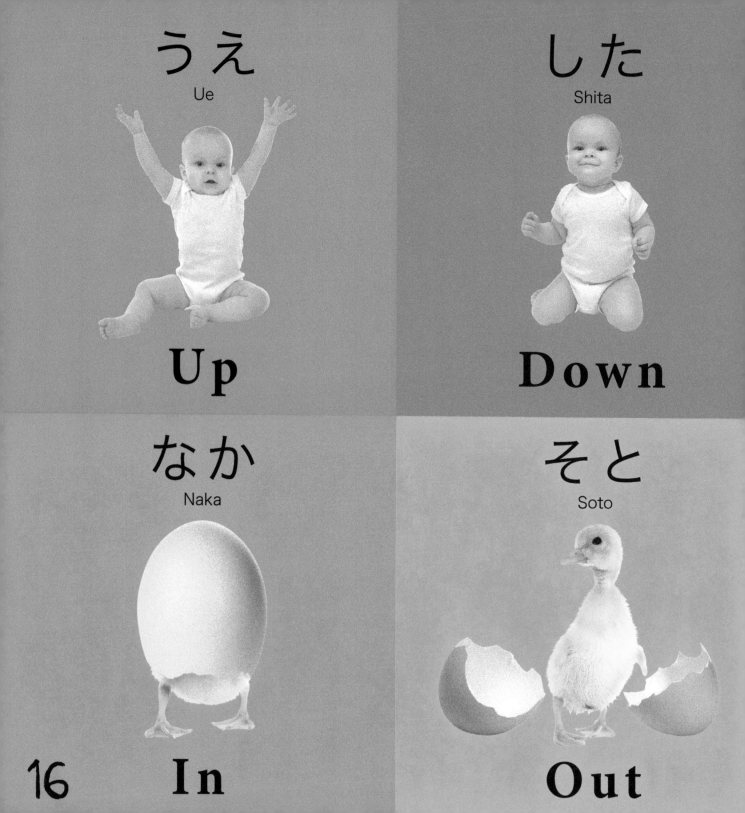

うえ
Ue

Up

した
Shita

Down

なか
Naka

16 **In**

そと
Soto

Out

あつい
Atsui

Hot

つめたい
Tsumetai

Cold

ぬれる
Nureru

Wet

かんそう
Kansō

Dry 17

まえ
Mae

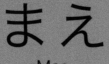

Front

うしろ
Ushiro

Back

おん
On

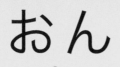

On

おふ
Ofu

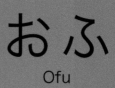

Off

18

あく

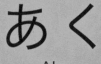

Open

とじる

Closed

から

Empty

まんぱい

Full

19

あんぜん
Anzen

Safe

きけん
Kiken

Dangerous

おおきい
Ookii

Big

ちいさい
Chiisai

Small

ねむる
Nemuru

Asleep

おきている
Okiteiru

Awake

ながい
Nagai

Long

みじかい
Mijikai

Short 21

まる

Maru

Circle

しかく
Shikaku

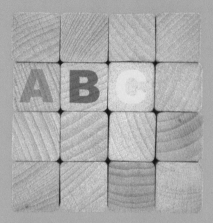

Square

さんかく
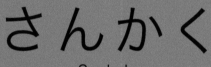
Sankaku

22 Triangle

ちょうほうけい
Chōhōkei

Rectangle

ひしがた
Hishigata

Diamond

ほしがた
Hoshigata

Star

だえんけい
Daenkei

Oval

はーとがた
Hātogata

Heart

23

くしゃみ
Kushami

はくしょん
Hakushon

Ah-choo

Sneeze

あひる
Ahiru

がー
Gā

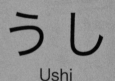

Quack

Duck

うし
Ushi

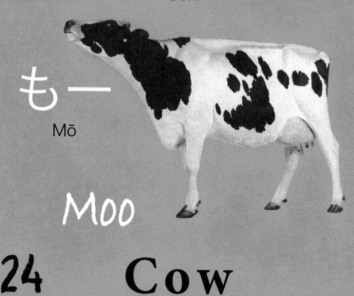

もー
Mō

Moo

24 **Cow**

でんわ
Denwa

じりりりり
Jiririririri

Rin

Phone

さる
Saru

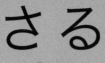

うっき
U-ki
うっき
u-ki

Ooh-
ooh-
ahh-
ahh

Monkey

かえる
Kaeru

けろけろ
Kerokero

Ribbit

Frog

しずか
Shizuka

しーっ
Shiiii

Shh

Hush 25

にわとり
Niwatori

こけこっこー
Kokekokkō

Cock-a-doodle-doo

Rooster

たいこ
Taiko

ばーん
Bān

Boom

Drums

へび
Hebi

しゃー
Shā

Hiss

Snake

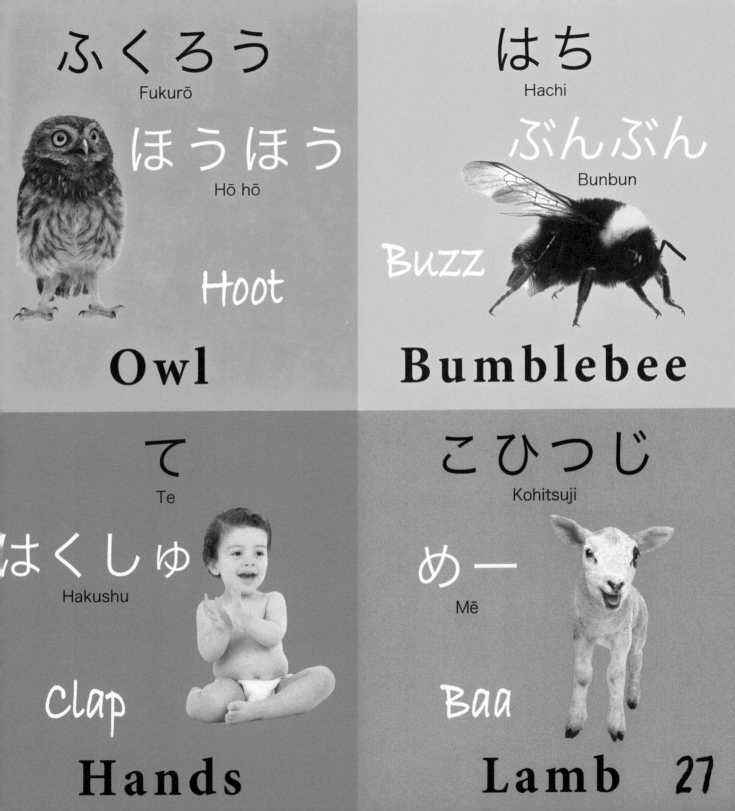

ふくろう
Fukurō

ほうほう
Hō hō

Hoot

Owl

はち
Hachi

ぶんぶん
Bunbun

Buzz

Bumblebee

て
Te

はくしゅ
Hakushu

Clap

Hands

こひつじ
Kohitsuji

めー
Mē

Baa

Lamb 27

はう
Hau

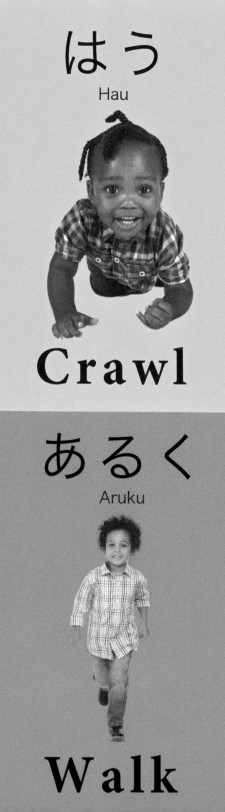

Crawl

ころがる
Korogaru

Roll

あるく
Aruku

Walk

はしる
Hashiru

Run

はねる
Haneru

Hop

のる
Noru

Ride

きす
Kisu

Kiss

とぶ
Tobu

Jump 29

うれしい
Ureshī

Happy

かなしい
Kanashī

Sad

おこる
Okoru

30 **Angry**

こわい
Kowai

Scared

いらいら
Iraira

Frustration

びっくり
Bikkuri

Surprise

しょうげき
Shōgeki

Shock

ゆうかん
Yūkan

Brave

31

やきゅう

Yakyū

Baseball

ばすけっとぼーる

Basuketto bo-ru

Basketball

てにす

Tenisu

32 Tennis

さっかー

Sakka

Soccer

ばどみんとん
Badminton

Badminton

あめふと
Ame futo

Football

ばれーぼーる
Bare- bo-ru

Volleyball

ごるふ
Gorufu

Golf

しょうぼうしゃ
Shi ~youbousha

Fire truck

くるま
Kuruma

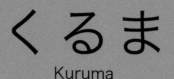

34 **Car**

とらっく
Torakku

Truck

Helicopter

ひこうき

Hikouki

Airplane

でんしゃ

Densha

Train

ふね

Fune

Boat 35

しょう
Shou

ちゅう
Chuu

だい
Dai

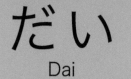

Small　　**Medium**　　**Large**

しょう
Shou

ちゅう
Chuu

だい
Dai

36 **Small**　　**Medium**　　**Large**

だい ちゅう しょう
Dai Chuu Shou

Large Medium Small

だい ちゅう しょう
Dai Chuu Shou

Large Medium Small 37

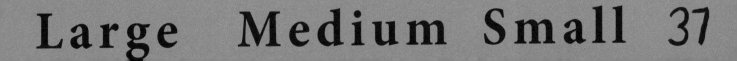

あたま
Atama

Head

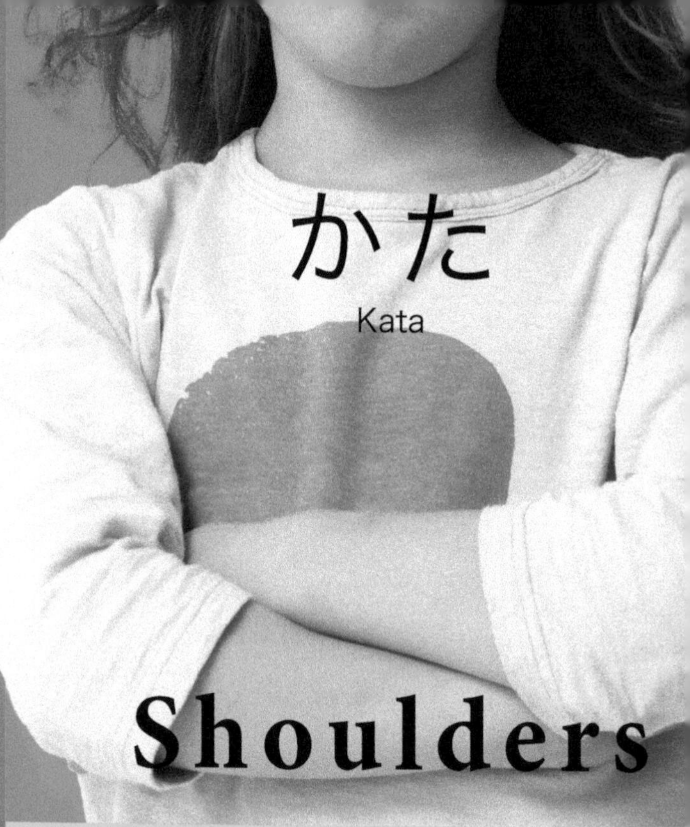

かた
Kata

Shoulders

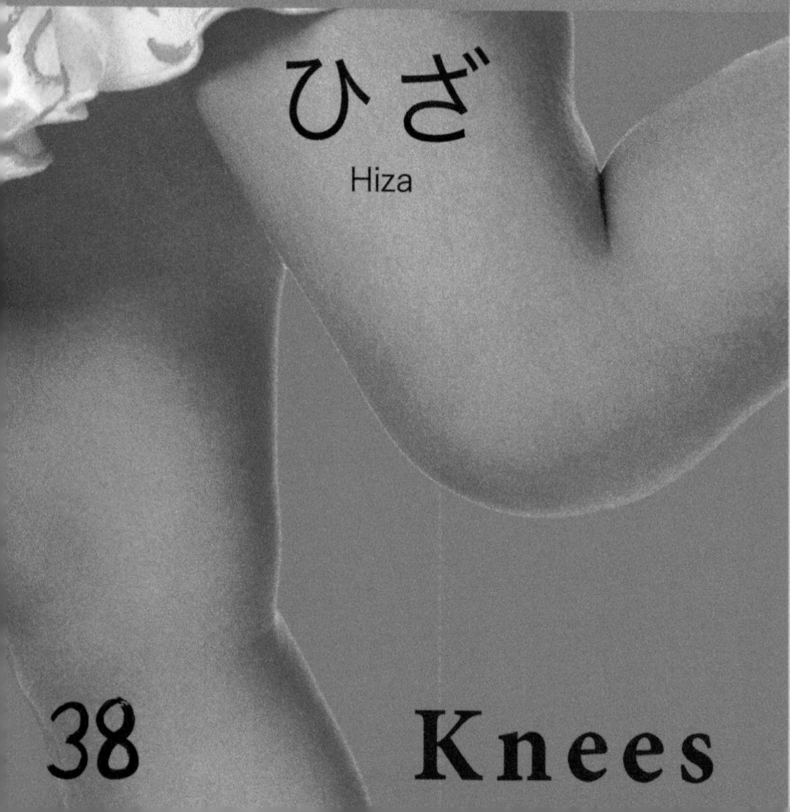

ひざ
Hiza

Knees

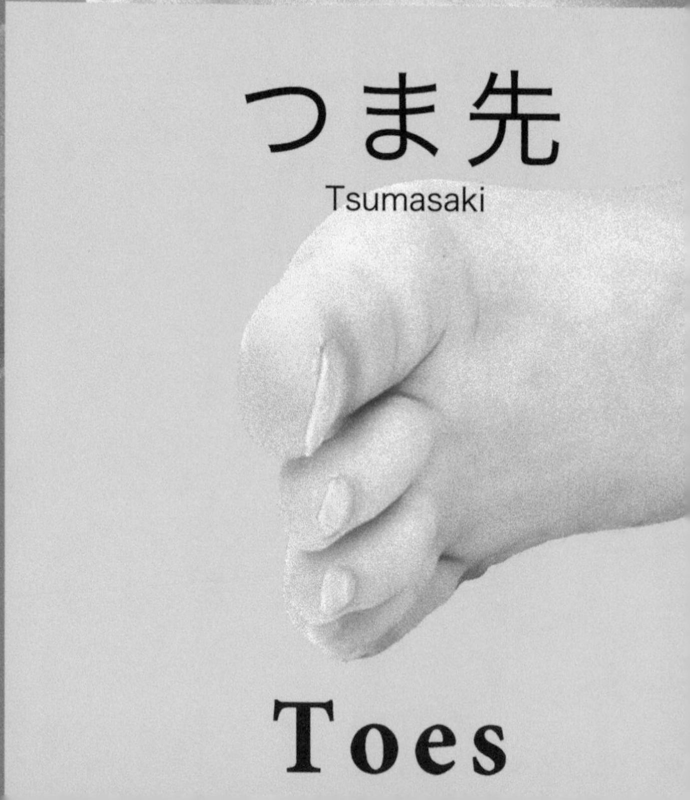

つま先
Tsumasaki

Toes

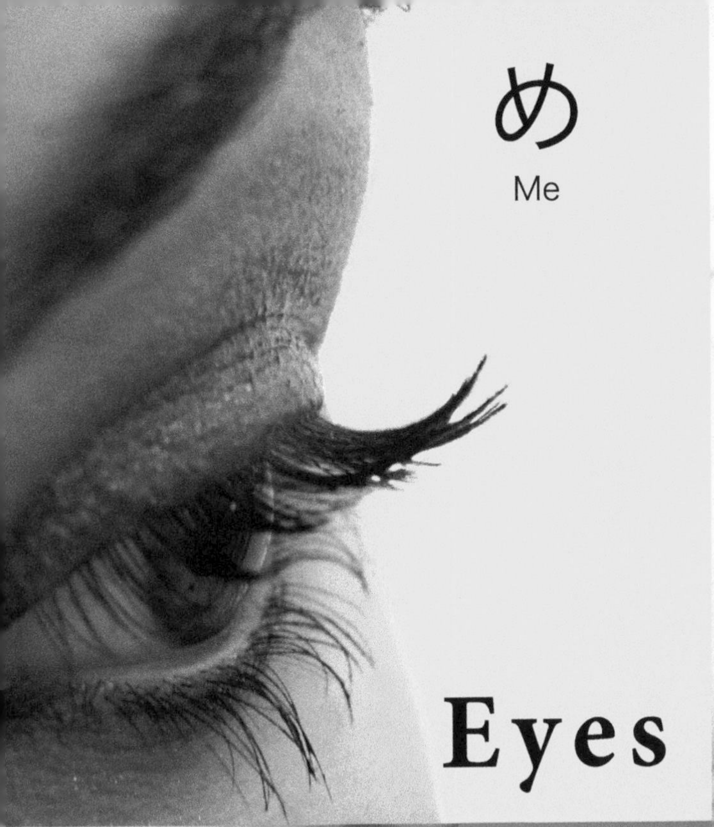

め
Me

Eyes

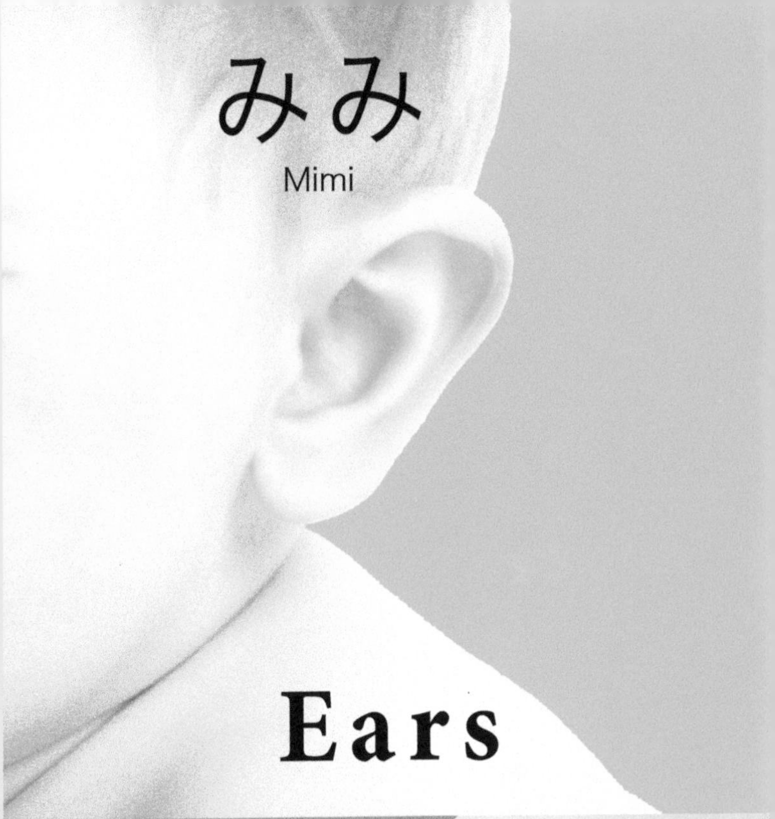

みみ
Mimi

Ears

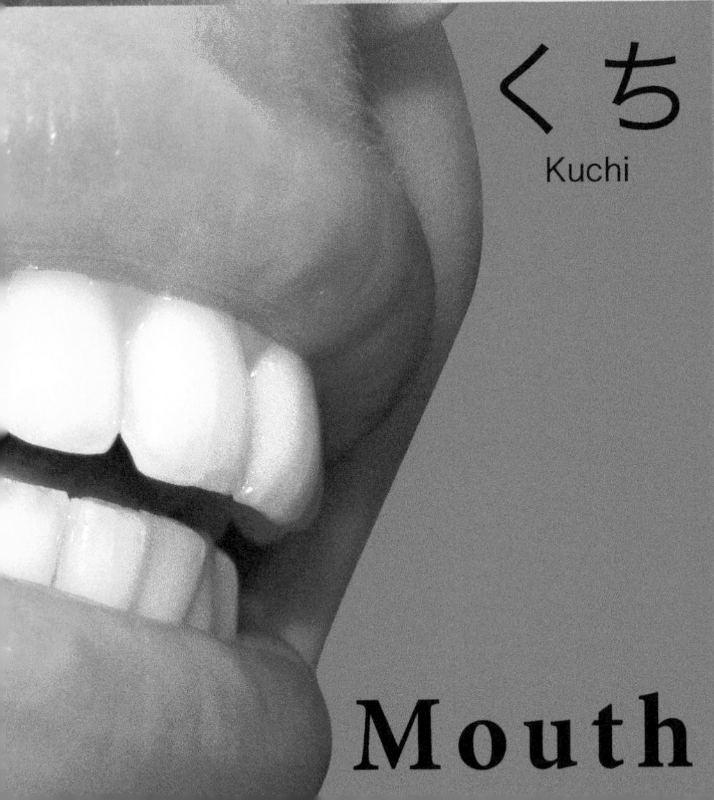

くち
Kuchi

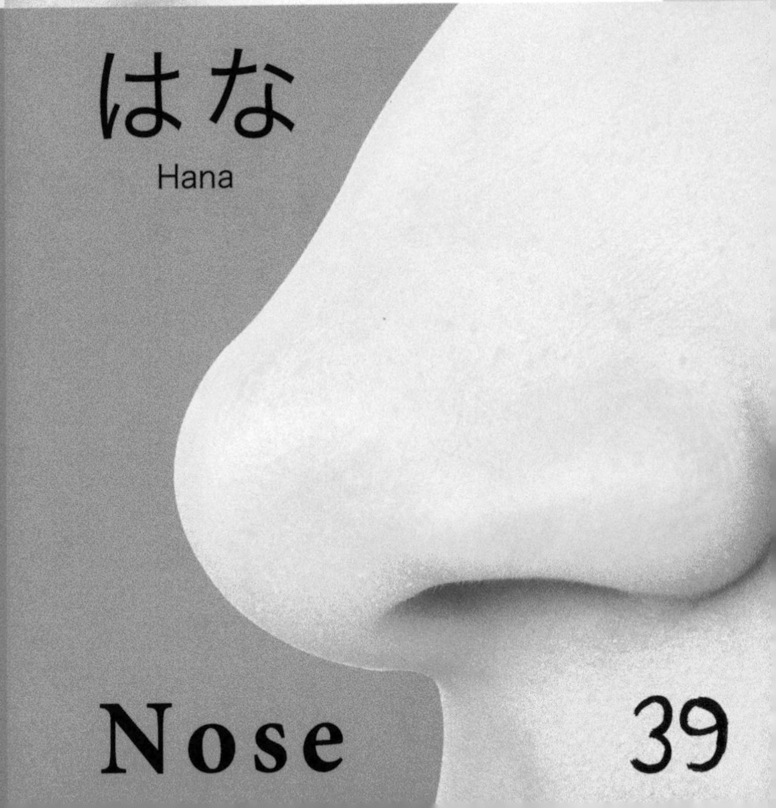

はな
Hana

Mouth **Nose**

べびーかっぷ
Bebīkappu

Sippy cup

おわん
Owan

Bowl

おなべ
Onabe

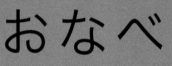

40 **Pot**

こっぷ
Koppu

Cup

おさら
Osara

Plate

ふぉーく
Fōku

Fork

ないふ
Naifu

Knife

さじ
Saji

Spoon

ぼうし
Bōshi

Hat

てぃーしゃつ
Te~ishatsu

Shirt

ずぼん
Zubon

Pants

たんぱん
Tanpan

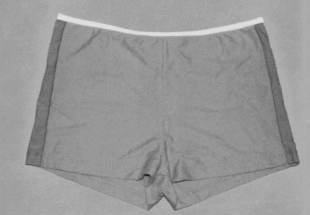

Shorts

てぶくろ
Tebukuro

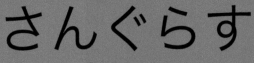

Gloves

さんぐらす
Sangurasu

Sunglasses

くつした
Kutsushita

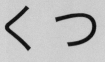

Socks

くつ
Kutsu

Shoes

43

おふろのじかん
Ofuro noji kan

おふろ
Ofuro

Bath time

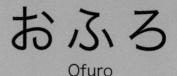

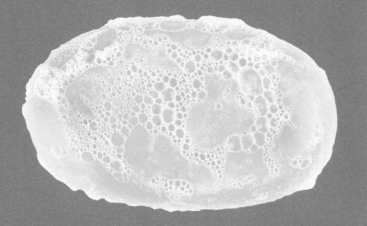

Bath

せっけん
Sekken

あひる
Ahiru

Soap

Rubber duck

はみがき
Hamigaki

Brush teeth

ねるじかん
Neruji kan

Bed time

ほん
Hon

Book

といれ
Toire

Potty

べっど
Beddo

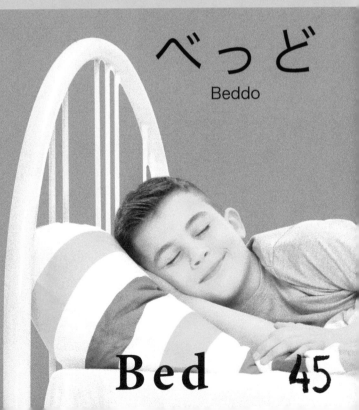

Bed

45

THE TODDLER'S handbOOk

activity / れんしゅう
Ren shū

Match the following to the pictures below. Can you find 7 pumpkins, a hooting owl, a rainbow, a baseball, a lion, square blocks, a sad boy, a helicopter, and shoes?

つぎのことばと、したのしゃしんをあわせましょう。あなたは、7つのかぼち
Tsugi no kotoba to, shita noshi ~yashinwoawasemashou. Anata wa, 7tsu no kabocha,

ないているふくろう、にじ、やきゅう、らいおん、せいほうけいのぶろっく、
Naite iru fukurō, niji, ya kyū,-ra ion, sei hō kei no buro kku,

かなしいおとこのこ、へりこぷたー、そしてくつをみつけることができますた
Kanashī o toko no ko, e Riko puta, soshite kutsu o mitsukeru koto ga dekimasu ka?

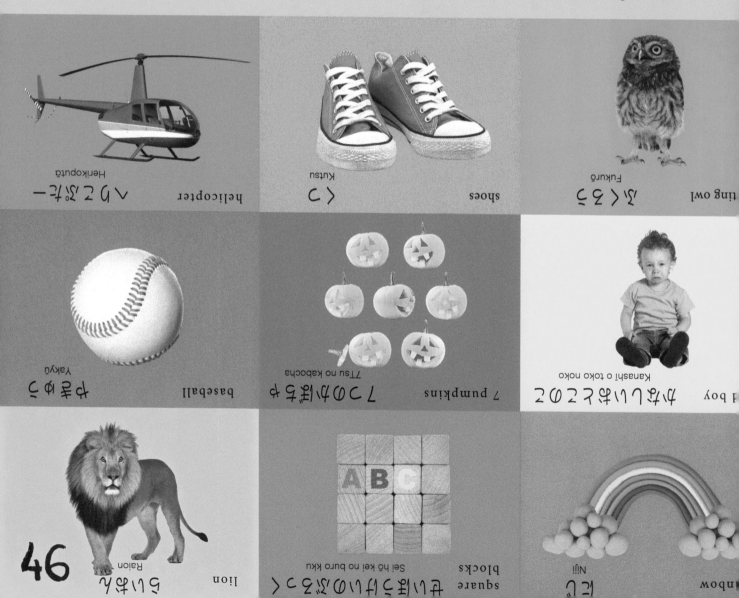

helicopter ヘリこぷたー Herikoputā

shoes くつ Kutsu

hooting owl ふくろう Fukurō

baseball やきゅう Yakyū

7 pumpkins 7つのかぼちゃ 7Tsu no kabocha

sad boy かなしいおとこのこ Kanashī o toko noko

lion らいおん Raion

square blocks せいほうけいのぶろっく Sei hō kei no buro kku

rainbow にじ Niji

46

Find more early concept books at www.engagebooks.ca

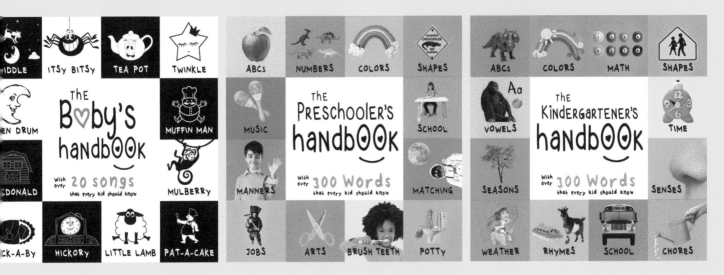

About the Author

Dayna Martin is the mother of three young boys. When she finished writing *The Toddler's Handbook* her oldest son was 18 months old, and she had newborn twins. Following the successful launch of her first book, Dayna began work on *The Baby's Handbook*, *The Preschooler's Handbook*, and *The Kindergartener's Handbook*. The ideas in her books were inspired by her search to find better ways to teach her children. The concepts were vetted by numerous educators in different grade levels. Dayna is a stay-at-home mom, and is passionate about teaching her children in innovative ways. Her experiences have inspired her to create resources to help other families. With thousands of copies sold, her books have already become a staple learning source for many children around the world.

Translations

ARABIC	JAPANESE
DUTCH	KOREAN
FILIPINO	MANDARIN
FRENCH	POLISH
GERMAN	PORTUGUESE
GREEK	RUSSIAN
HEBREW	SPANISH
HINDI	VIETNAMESE
ITALIAN	

Have comments or suggestions?
Contact us at: alexis@engagebooks.ca

Show us how you enjoy your #handbook. Tweet a picture to @engagebooks for a chance to win free prizes.